IMAGES
of England

BURNLEY

Daniel Drew, 1880s, taking a photograph.

IMAGES
of England

BURNLEY

Compiled by
Michael Townend

TEMPUS

First published 1999
Copyright © Michael Townend, 1999

Tempus Publishing Limited
The Mill, Brimscombe Port,
Stroud, Gloucestershire, GL5 2QG

ISBN 0 7524 1566 2

Typesetting and origination by
Tempus Publishing Limited
Printed in Great Britain by
Midway Clark Printing, Wiltshire

To Sam and Sophie whose history is in the future.

James Pilkington (left), nicknamed 'Silly Jimmy' and 'Jimmy Gannow Top' was photographed here in the 1880s probably at Gannow. Little more is known of him.

Contents

Acknowledgements

Thanks to Ken Spencer, James Howell and Roger Frost for advising on historical accuracy.

I am also indebted to the following for their help during the preparation of this book: Lancashire County Library (East Lancashire Division – Reference and Local Studies Department), North West Sound Archive, *Burnley Express*, *Lancashire Evening Telegraph*, East Lancashire Medal and Militaria Society, Manx National Heritage, Barbara Bailey, Barbara Bolton, Susan Bourne, Graham Briggs, Ivy Buckley, Noel Coates, Marie Durning, Sarah Fergusson, Edward Gibbons, Cllr John Greenwood JP, Molly Haines, Dr Michael Harrison, Dr Tony Kitto, Graham Lawlor, John Monk, Kathleen Slade, Claire Stewart, Carol Stinton, Karen Townend.

Introduction

Anyone can study local history; it is full of 'characters', events, opinions and tragedies. It is also fun. We are studying people who may seem totally different to ourselves and yet their history has shaped and continues to shape our own lives, where we live, what we do and how we plan the future. Many today may regret the loss of a perceived sense of community and discipline but we have also largely lost massive infant mortality, insanitary housing and conditions, poor diet and reduced life expectancy.

The town of Burnley is an example of this. Set in the Brun and Calder valley, Burnley was a loose collection of settlements surrounded by moorland. Development was slow until rapid growth (as with other towns in Lancashire and Yorkshire) was created by the textile industry. Originally based on wool, this was superseded by cotton spinning, then weaving. Cotton was supported by coal mining and engineering as well as a relatively small calico printing trade. Successful industrialists, wealthy people and those less wealthy helped shape the town. This ranged from developing the mill village at Lowerhouse to involvement in local government and social concerns such as the Victoria Hospital.

The photographs show the town during this period of creation, direction and change, from 1850-1960. They come from the collection at Towneley Hall Art Gallery and Museum, the town's museum since 1903. This collection consists of lithographic views, paintings, photographic prints, family portraits, 'snapshots', postcards, glass positives and negatives. The photographers' names are mostly unknown, although a few can be identified including James Thornber, Friend Robinson and Daniel Drew. The first was a cotton manufacturer and James clearly thought about the composition of his photographs, as at Towneley railway station (see p. 95). He also reacted quickly to events, recording the disaster at Dick Boys' shop (p. 46), Lodge Mill fire (p. 74), and to use his words, the 'boiler that blew up out the Meadows into the Cross Keys bedroom' (p. 75). Friend Robinson was based in Parliament Street and his prints can be recognized by both their paper and tone. Daniel Drew left a relatively small, but nevertheless important series of photographs of Lowerhouse Printworks for the period 1880-1912. It is incomplete because the photographs of the steam engine are missing. He boxed the glass plates according to the year they were photographed. In some cases he gave the exact date they were taken (p. 82).

Thornber also dated some images, but as in the case of the boiler explosion, the historian has to use other sources of information to determine a date. Concerning the boiler explosion, a newspaper of March 1892 gave a vivid description: 'the astonished crowd were gazing helpless with dread at the unusual aerolite...... it came down rapidly towards the earth and dropped upon the rear portion of the roof of the Cross Keys Inn and crashed into the bedroom'. A large crowd gathered to 'where the unusual sky rocket had alighted'. In this case, the newspaper article can be used directly with the image.

In other cases, photographs of a street scene often have street furniture, street names, public houses, shops, bill posters, churches, schools, factories and costumeas clues. These can be used in conjunction with other sources to help arrive at a date. These sources include trade directories, newspapers, obituaries, maps and advertisements. Dating a photograph will almost inevitably provide additional information. Colne Road (p. 57) is an example of the various sources which can be used to arrive at a date.

Despite having all these sources and modern retrieval systems, there are still some images which people know little about (as with James Pilkington, see p. 4). In such cases, the use of family and oral history often helps. Interest in these has increased massively over the past few years and people's descriptions of events, scenes and personalities, although subjective, give different perspectives and can also be compared to contemporary descriptions.

Messages on the rear of postcards give personal insights. They may range from 'having a nice time' to others which touch on social issues. One good example is in the collection at Towneley – written during the September break in 1906, the card was sent from Nelson to Blackpool (not vice versa as we might expect) to a weaver lodging with a landlady. The picture is of a weaving shed and the message refers to the fact that the holidaymaker's 'clogs and fent (apron\overall) are straving (starving) for the want of work. If you don't give over talking to these pen darters (pen pushers) you may have to keep single all your life'.

I hope you enjoy this selection of photographs from the local collections at Towneley Hall. We are always pleased to help with enquiries.

Michael Townend
Towneley Hall
Burnley

One
Towneley Hall and Park

Towneley Hall, 1920s. The historic home of the Towneley family from the mid-thirteenth century, the Hall was opened as Burnley's public art gallery and museum in 1903; there had previously been private clubs, rooms and societies. The park had been opened a year earlier than the art gallery and museum. The German cannon was placed outside the entrance after the First World War but was removed in October 1930, when there was a general anti-war feeling.

Richard Henry Towneley. Richard was the last male heir of the Towneley family but he died of a fever in Rome in 1877 before he could inherit Towneley and the estates. The inheritance was eventually divided between co-heiresses, with the Hall passing to Alice Mary Towneley, Lady O'Hagan. She was the last resident before the Hall was opened as a museum.

A rear view of Towneley Hall, c. 1900. On the ground floor is the Great Hall and above it were the family bedrooms and nursery which were to later become the art galleries. In the early years of the museum, Sunday afternoon concerts were held on the grass, with a sheet opened out for the public to donate money to the band who were playing. The area behind the photographer was known as the 'wilderness'.

Servants at Towneley Hall, *c.* 1859. During the nineteenth century the Towneley family mainly employed female staff. Most were born outside the district, coming from such towns as Harbottle (Northumberland) and Attleborough (Norfolk). Many worked at the Hall for short periods, often leaving to marry local men. Ann Champ (far left) was born in 1836 at Lulworth (Dorset). She was in service there and was reputedly invited to work at Towneley by a member of the family, on account of her cakes and pastries. While at Towneley, she met and married carpenter Francis Stuttard and they lived at Organ Row on Hufling Lane. The Towneleys also employed gamekeepers, land agents and stockmen as well as renting out land to tenant farmers.

Hanbrig Castle or Handbridge House, Todmorden Road. This was built for Charles Townley during 1797 and 1798 at a cost of £687. The building was intended to provide an impressive entrance into the main carriageway leading to the Hall and was occupied by Towneley land agents, Thomas Forshaw and Edward Lovat. In 1888, the entrance through the gate was described as 'not like the road to Silas Marner's cottage through nutty hedgerows but how charmed we are, how it opens our inward eye, what a feeling of peace creeps over us'. The castle was bought by the Corporation in the 1920s but fell into decay and was demolished in 1958.

Hanbrig Castle looking towards Todmorden Road. Burnley Wood developed in the mid to late nineteenth century with new communities and factories built on agricultural land to the east of the canal. Opposite Hanbrig was Spa Field Mill, one of the factories clustered around Oxford Road and Parliament Street. Behind Spa Field was Burnley Wood Mill, the scene of rioting in 1878. The Mayor wrote to the local military commander: 'There is a riot in Burnley. Therefore I read the riot act at 6.20 p.m. today. Now in as so much the civil authorities are unable to quell the disturbance, I am under the necessity of calling in your aid'. Spa Field Mill was to have been a temporary mortuary in the Second World War if there were large casualties due to bombing.

Causeway End, 1920s. The farm was occupied by the Crain family, long-time tenant farmers of the Towneleys. The spoil heap on the left fronted Todmorden Road and was from the Towneley Colliery. Coal was collected here by the unemployed in the 1930s. 'My dad taught me to pick coal. We both had a little pick each and used to scratch at the tip and if we were lucky we might get a bag now and then.'

Towneley café in the 1920s. The café, or 'refreshment rooms', was in the smaller of two stable blocks by 1906. The larger block to the right (not visible) was demolished in June 1951. Also at this time, alterations were made inside the café; partitions were removed on the ground floor and a second dining room created upstairs.

The gardens looking towards the site of the War Memorial. The large oak tree in the foreground and the cedar of Lebanon, behind, were probably planted in 1803 by Charles Townley. He planted both native and ornamental trees and was responsible for changing the garden from a formal style to an informal landscape garden overlooking the surrounding countryside by means of unobtrusive ha-ha walls. Previously there was an enclosed orchard on this site.

Wreath-laying at the memorial, 1928. The War Memorial was unveiled on 12 December 1926 and was paid for by the bequest of Caleb Thornber, a former mayor. Over 30,000 people attended the unveiling to pay tribute to over 4,000 men who died as a result of the Great War. Relatives waited over two hours to lay wreaths. David MacLean who served in the Royal Army Medical Corps laid the wreath in 1928.

Foldys Cross, *c.* 1908. The cross was originally erected in St Peter's churchyard in 1520 over the grave of John Foldys, chantry priest. The cross was partly destroyed in 1789 and re-erected behind the Hall. It was moved again in 1911 to the top of Lime Walk. The war memorial in St Peter's churchyard was modelled on the cross and unveiled in 1920.

Towneley Rustic Bridge, Upper Wood

Rustic bridge. This bridge became one of the features in the park. The Corporation developed other amenities such as the tennis court and bowling green at Causeway End which were opened in 1924. Causeway End farm was adapted as part of the municipal golf course. Cottages were built in 1929 for employees, shelters were erected and footpaths created. Environmental work has been undertaken since the 1980s.

Lady O'Hagan with members of family and associates, c. 1886. The group is shown outside the Hall and they consist of, from left to right: Thomas O'Hagan, -?-, -?-, Mademoiselle Briand (French governess), Lady O'Hagan, Mary and Maurice O'Hagan, -?-, Kathleen O'Hagan, Coquette the goat. After the division of the Towneley estates, Lady O'Hagan lived in the Hall. She became interested in many aspects of social and educational work, served on the Local Education Committee, was a County Magistrate and President of the Ladies' Committee of the Victoria Hospital. She supported the League of Social Services, opening a school for mothers in 1914 which was hoped would reduce the mortality rate. Schoolchildren lined the funeral route to Holme when she died in November 1921.

William T. Taylor, July 1913. William's work as a prominent electrical engineer involved travel all over the world. Between 1908 and 1913, he sent exhibits from Mexico, Peru, Egypt and Kashmir to Towneley Hall to be displayed. Some Kashmiri embroideries were made especially for the museum and exhibits were displayed in a 'W.T. Taylor' room.

The Great Hall, 1890s. During the late Victorian period, the hall had a stove, billiard table, screens and aspidistras. The baroque plasterwork is by Francesco Vassalli and Martino Quadri. The builder for these alterations made in the 1720s was Robert Thornton of York. The sculpture is a copy of the classical sculpture, the *Laocoon*, in the Vatican. When the museum opened, the Great Hall was used to display various items including Egyptology. 'I was fascinated and repelled by a mummy which was on display, I would dream about it for a week. There was also a life sized stuffed bear and an elephant's skull.'

The Long Gallery, 1930s. The gallery was used to display seventeenth century furniture purchased from Needham's of Manchester, African antlers from benefactor Captain Astley's collection, weapons and drums. The aspidistras and palms were probably supplied by the Parks Department. An illustration of 1835 shows the gallery more sparsely furnished with high-backed chairs, chests, and family portraits incorporated into the panelling above the guest bedrooms on the right. The Towneleys and their guests, apparently, used the Long Gallery for exercise during bad weather. There were pleasant views at both ends.

Edward Stocks Massey, *c.* 1904. Edward was from the brewing family. He bequeathed over £100,000 to the Corporation for the benefit of arts and education. As early as 1904, it had been recognized that the museum had little money for purchasing exhibits and the Stocks Massey bequest helped purchase a large number of items, particularly paintings. The bequest also helped (and continues to help) other organizations and projects in the town.

Two
Buildings

St James's Street, 1920s. The BSK café (named after owners Brown, Sutcliffe and Kellett) was opened in December 1908. Cakes were made in the basement in ovens 'large enough to roast a bull'. Outside the BSK the area was known as 'the drag', a meeting place for single people. A similar area was the 'chicken run' on Colne Road. The BSK closed in June 1961.

The Craven Bank, Hargreaves Street. Economic crisis followed the failure of a local bank run by the Holgates in 1824. Soon after, a bank run by Alcock, Birkbeck & Co. took over the work of the Holgates. Alcock, Birkbeck & Co. opened the Craven Bank between Coal Street and St James's Row in the 1850s.

The Lancashire and Yorkshire Bank, Hargreaves Street. The first branch of this bank was opened in 1874. The site in Hargreaves Street was bought in 1885 and the new branch opened in 1886. The fittings were made by local companies such as Collinge's, the furniture makers, who also made the manager's desk. The upper floors were let to other tenants.

St James's Street, *c.* 1905. In 1889 it had been reported that fifty-six licensed houses were within a radius of 300 yards of the Market Hall. The number of public houses caused concern among the Temperance Movement but children often made them the subject of games, 'we would play at remembering what the next pub would be named after. A bird, or animal, or tree. The Royal Oak, Dog and Duck, Thorn Hotel, Red Lion, White Lion …' The Boot, White Lion and Clock Face were all rebuilt in 1911. The shops between them were Easton's (brushes), Slater's (tripe and pies) and a saddler's which is hidden from view. A greengrocer's was between the White Lion and Parker Lane.

Old Sparrow Hawk Inn, Church Street, *c.* 1899. T' Church Inn or The Old Sparrow Hawk was probably the oldest named pub, built in the fifteenth century. The name derives from the crest of the Towneley family as it was originally the Towneley Arms. The inn, with St Peter's church opposite, was at the centre of the town ('Top o'th'Town) - until the nineteenth century. The market and fair was held here and the stocks and market cross were outside the inn. The last resident was Sarah Whitham and the pub was demolished in 1890 to be replaced by a new building; Ormerod Road on the left replaced Godley Lane.

Corporation Arms, Curzon Street, *c.* 1935. Originally a private house, the inn was owned by the Corporation. It was run from around 1860 to 1967 (when it closed) by three generations of the Wilkinson family, all of whom were called James. It was demolished soon after closing. The advertising signs were painted by Alf Smith (see p.87).

The Woodman Inn, Todmorden Road. Three cottages were rebuilt as the Woodman public house. The name was one of several similar ones in Burnley Wood, the others being the Owl in the Wood and the Cottage in the Wood. The sign outside reputedly showed William Gladstone dressed as a woodman. The public house was rebuilt in 1914 on the corner of Todmorden Road and Oxford Road for Fernandes's Old Brewery of Bridge Street.

Old Red Lion, Manchester Road, *c.* 1890. The Red Lion was originally a farm but by the early 1800s there was a brewhouse, stables and shippon. The inn was used by general carriers as well as being a coaching inn for Manchester. The building and land was purchased by the Corporation and the pub was demolished, being rebuilt in 1868. The site was considered for the Town Hall but this was rejected.

The Bull and Butcher Inn, Manchester Road, 1898. The public house on the former turnpike road to Manchester was rebuilt in 1913. Sporting events were sometimes held on land nearby including wrestling matches and running. When a car park was laid at the rear in 1989, clay pipe bowls and stems were found. One of the last people to make clay pipes, in around 1895, lived in a cottage next to the pub.

Rosie Bannister. Rosie was a member of the Salvation Army and was a 'reformed' character. The Temperance Movement was strong in the town and was closely linked to church and chapel, 'we would be told a pure God fearing non boozer had shown he could thread ten needles whilst the boozer was still trying to pick the needle up'.

St Leonard's church, Church Street, Padiham, 1866. The first reference to a church here was in 1451 when there was probably a chantry chapel on this site. St Leonard's is thought to have been built in the early sixteenth century and rebuilt in 1766. However, by the 1860s it was too small for the growing population. The church was demolished and the foundation stone for the new building laid in 1866. The stone was laid by a member of the Starkie family of Huntroyde who had a long association with the church. The new church was opened in January 1869.

St Peter's church and school, Church Street, c. 1864. The first documentary evidence for the church was in 1122 when it was one of three in the parish of Whalley. It was rebuilt in 1533 and saw restorations in 1789, 1854 and 1992. A Sunday school had been opened in Dawson Square (opposite the church) in 1787. Forty-one years later, St Peter's National School was opened; this was the town's first day-school and it was run by Thomas Carus. It was supported by fees and collections made in church. A description of school life prior to 1839 stated: 'we opened with the hymn "The Lord He makes the sun to know" and closed with "And now another day is gone". On a quiet afternoon our singing could be heard at Brennand Mill'. On the bottom right of the photograph can be seen the stocks, known to have been last used in 1853.

Holy Trinity church, Accrington Road. The church was built in 1836 as a 'Commissioners Church' to a design by Lewis Vulliamy. A fund was set up for new churches where congregations were expanding. Holy Trinity was one of eighty-one built in Lancashire by the fund. The last service was held in 1989 and the church sold for conversion to flats in 1992.

Brunswick chapel, Manchester Road. The chapel was built over the River Calder and opened in 1869. The novelist Silas Hocking, author of *Her Benny*, was minister between 1876 and 1879. As with so many chapels and churches, Brunswick was a focus for the community. There were rambling, cycling and swimming clubs, and table tennis, football and cricket teams. The cricketers were 'the strongest in the league and held up all the others by holding the bottom position'. The chapel was demolished in 1963.

Coal Clough school, *c.* 1903. Prior to 1870, education had been haphazard but the Education Act in that year led to compulsory education. Areas were divided into districts managed by School Boards and schools were built where they were needed. These included Abel Street (1891) and Coal Clough (1900). One pupil who enrolled was Mabel ? (second row, fourth from left) who sent this photograph to her father serving in the Navy. According to one child at Coal Clough, on 'windy days we would let the wind blow us down Ulster Street to school. For playtime eats I took oatmeal and sugar in an envelope'. The furniture was probably made in Padiham, where there were three school furniture makers in the early 1900s.

Carlton Road school (Grant's school), c. 1890. The school was founded by William Milner Grant in 1861. William was probably one of the most influential teachers of his time and many of the town's leading figures attended here. Shortly after William's death in 1888, former students founded a scholarship to the Grammar School which was open to all public elementary schools in the town. A plaque recording this hung for many years in Room One of the Grammar School. William's headstone in St Peter's churchyard was also erected by old scholars 'in token of their appreciation of his earnest teaching, fatherly counsel and noble example'. The school closed in 1901 and was demolished soon after. At a reunion, former pupils recalled the moral as well as academic teaching with the 'abhorrence of wrongdoing, firm adherence to the truth'. Hence the school motto, *Recte Agere Aude* (dare to do what is right).

Carlton Road school, c. 1894. Pupils came from Nelson and Padiham as well as Burnley and by the 1890s girls were admitted. Subjects covered included Ireland, London (capital of the British Empire), specific gravity and the Battle of Waterloo. Each year the school had a picnic and in 1894 some pupils went to Hurst Green. Here they played cricket, had tea and stopped at Whalley on their return.

Grammar School, Bank Parade. The school was founded in 1559 and gave a limited number of scholars a classical education. The school occupied several sites until the 1874 building was erected on Bank Parade. This was used until 1959 when a new grammar school was opened at Habergham.

Technical School, Ormerod Road, 1934. The building was opened in September 1909 to accommodate over 2,000 day and evening scholars in total, as well as a weaving college and Girls' High School. The first High School magazine of 1911 reported that furnishing was sparse and in some places floorboards were not laid.

Girls' High School cookery class, 1934. The first principal at the High School was Miss Louisa Wood followed by Miss Dorothy Howard. During 1934, Miss Howard and other teachers organized trips to a Manchester theatre, to a newspaper, as well as enjoying a lantern lecture on the solar system. Clubs at school included folk dancing, chess, a League of Nations union, debating, literary and dramatic societies as well as the school orchestra.

Triumphal Arch, Church Street, October 1886, built when Prince Albert visited the town to open the Victoria Hospital. It was the first royal visit since 1323 and Burnley was decorated with flags, banners, flowers and arches. One of the most impressive was the one shown here, in Church Street close to the Well Hall Brewery. Over seventy feet high, it was decorated with flags, evergreens and fabrics.

Victoria Hospital, *c.* 1890. Opened in 1886, the hospital was built and maintained by subscription and fund-raising, started in 1883. The circular wards were called 'Butterworth' and 'Thursby' after ardent supporters, and on opening the hospital, commemorative medallions and plates were made. The hospital was supported by fund-raising until the founding of the National Health Service in 1948.

The opening of the children's ward, Victoria Hospital, July 1891. There was a need for a separate children's ward and an appeal was set up to raise £3,000. Subscriptions were raised with a committee under Lady O'Hagan providing the balance. Designed by the local firm, Waddington & Son, the ward had twenty beds and a footpath outside was provided for 'convalescent inmates'.

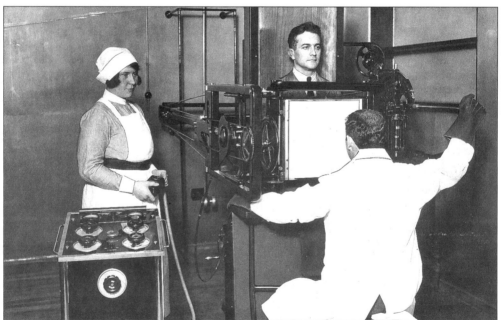

The X-ray department, Victoria Hospital, January 1932. The first X-ray machinery had been provided by Sir John O.S. Thursby. New equipment was purchased in 1932, again with the help of benefactors. The radioscopic room was where the screen examinations were made. This machine was the teleorthscope, used by the radiologist to examine inside the body.

Three
Shopping

Yorkshire Street, *c.* 1927. All these buildings have now been demolished. On the right was the Sion Baptist chapel and shops leading to the Hall Inn at the bottom. On the left, shops included Crook's (clothier) as well as a butcher, a confectioner, milliner, newsagent and the larger Premier Billiards Hall.

Market Hall interior, *c*. 1874. The foundation stone of the hall was laid in 1866 on land replacing shambles and properties run by the Burnley Market Company. To accommodate the new structure, several buildings were demolished, streets levelled and some of the worst insanitary properties in the town removed. Designed by James Green, the building was opened in 1870 under the control of the Corporation. Stalls were added outside including a fish market. During the 1870s, businesses inside (aside from James Winskill, confectioner) included John Simpson (basket and skip maker), Lupton's (bookseller), butchers, glass and china, fancy goods and hardware dealers. The market remained gaslit until 1950 when electricity was introduced but only until 1966 when the building was demolished. It was replaced by the current Market Hall, opened in 1970.

Market day, c. 1909. Stalls were both inside and outside the Market Hall, 'Sunday morning was spent playing on the market, swinging on the iron work of the fish stalls and jumping from one to the other. We would go feeling down the holes that they used to stick poles in for the stalls and found many a shilling'.

Howe Street, (Market Place) *c.* 1880. Directly opposite the Market Hall was Weston's which was a confectioner's and restaurant, Dickinson's grocers and Altham's tea merchants and grocers. Abraham Altham started organizing rail excursions to the seaside in 1874. Tickets for the trips were sold from his shops; it proved successful and the travel business eventually took over from the tea trade.

Market Street, *c.* 1908. Alfred Cooper's (tripe dealers) was next to Wigglesworth's (draper) and Brown's (watchmaker). Cooper's had previously been occupied by a shop selling baby clothes. It was later occupied by Ralph Mason's (also a tripe dresser) with Dearden's milliners and Charlie Clegg's sports outfitters next door. These shops, where business was conducted over a counter, were typical of the time; 'walk round stores' were opened much later.

Walter Porrett's grocers, Chancery Street, *c.* 1896. Walter (left) opened his own shop in 1888, after having worked at a shop in the Market Place. He was president of the local Grocers' Association, 1920-22. Walter died in 1923 but the shop remained a family business, priding itself on the selection of ham, bacon and cheese.

Bank of England, Brown Street. This was a small shop owned by Councillor Robinson Place. In 1929 the sign was removed by order of the official Bank of England. The origin of the sign is unknown. It was suggested that it had been part of the Commercial Bank of England, yet 'no one has ever burgled the premises in the belief that bullion was concealed in the cellars, nor has anyone faced the occupier with a thousand pound note'.

Horatio Hartley on his ninetieth birthday. Horatio started out as a butcher in around 1829 on Market Street. During the 1842 Plug Riots, 'all the shops in the neighbourhood were demanded of their contents. The crowd made a special design upon Mr Hartley's shop, being well stocked with meat, he and his brother armed themselves with knives and kept back the plunderers. The mob deemed it prudent to leave his shop alone'.

The Co-operative Central Stores, Hammerton Street, 1890s. The shops came to dominate Hammerton Street with premises on both sides dealing with everything from jewellery to shoe repairers and furnishing. As general manager, James Ashworth (centre) was largely responsible for increasing membership in the movement from 1,000 in 1882 to over 12,000 in 1901. There were branches throughout the town but visitors to the Central Stores in 1897 were 'surprised to see the amount of business done in one single hour let alone what must be done during the whole of a week'. The movement, as well as providing customers with their 'divis', was involved with welfare and education. It also advocated improved rights for women through the Co-operative Women's Guild.

'Burnley's latest wonder', 1930s. This was the Co-operative Society's travelling grocer's shop. Herbert Berry, Jim Tattersall and Jim Maddran (?) were 'going to save the housewife tiresome journeys. A grocer's shop full of a great variety of goods fresh from our wonderful Central Store will drive up to your door – not "Any orders today" but "Here we are today".'

John Mackenzie,(or 'Long de Dong'), a street trader. He could be heard in the streets in the 1860s shouting 'Long de Dong' as he looked for customers to buy his matches. He was easily recognized by his hat, muffler, basket and stick but it 'was rather dangerous for mischievous youths to tease him and get within reach; they would learn that the peddlers stick was thicker and harder than their heads'.

John Baldwin ('Cheap John'). John owned Cheap John's bazaar on Hammerton Street, one of several shops in the town selling low price goods. He eventually moved to America and the shop was demolished in 1924, the same year as Woolworths opened on the opposite side of the street.

Collinge's, Hammerton Street. The furniture company was started by Luke Collinge in the 1840s and was carried on by his sons, William and John. The shop had showrooms and 'fifteen artistically decorated specimen rooms' showing furniture made by John. In 1924 the building was taken over by Woolworths whose prices were under sixpence for everything from sweets to paint and enamelware.

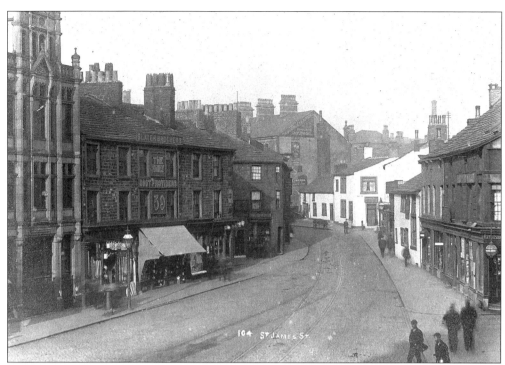

St James's Street, *c.* 1892. The narrow street was hemmed in by buildings. On the left was Cowgill and Smith (ironmonger), Slater's (boots), Kippax (woollen), Harker's ironmonger (makers of washing possers) and Robert Munn's (chemist and registrar). The street was widened in 1905 with the demolition of some of these buildings. The broadest point was then opposite the Boot Inn (behind the bollard) giving a clear view from Manchester Road to Yorkshire Street.

Hepworth's, St James's Street, *c.* 1890. Hepworth's was one of the few shops not run by a local family. The Leeds clothing firm occupied the premises for a few years around 1890. Thereafter, it continued in use as a clothing shop. On the right is the Thorn Hotel, one of the most popular inns in the town.

Dick Boys' shop, January 1896. The premises were in Brown Street in the area known as 'Bottom o'th'Town'. The chimney and part of the Bottom o'th'Town mill collapsed and the shop 'was simply crushed like an eggshell beneath the tons of precipitating material'. Dick and his wife, Rebecca, were unfortunately killed in the accident; a relief fund for their children was quickly established.

St James's Street, c. 1924. The shops between Bethesda Street and Brown Street were demolished in 1925 to widen the street and allow a new block to be built. Several names were suggested for the new building including Bethesda and Victoria, until Empire Buildings was decided upon. The new block contained a boot and shoe dealer, a milliner, outfitter and tailor.

St James's Street, 1920s. The Blue Clock buildings on the right were formerly occupied by Hepworth's (see p. 45). Shops in the row included Dolcis, Slater and Slater (boots and shoes), Flack (mantles), a stay maker, The White Horse public house and Richard Hargreaves (tea and coffee). Those on the opposite side included Frank Pick (chemist) and Burton's, occupying St James's Hall with the clock tower. All the buildings on the right have been demolished. When Hargreaves's Big Wheel shop was demolished in 1965, items were donated to Towneley Hall's collection including packaging, signs, and containers as well as the Big Wheel coffee grinder.

Manchester Road, 1902. By the early nineteenth century the centre of the town had 'moved' to what is now St James's Street and the bottom of Manchester Road. The Bull Hotel, formerly a farmhouse, was rebuilt in 1817 as Burnley's premier hotel. Stagecoaches operated from here and it was the venue for many social events. The building was demolished in 1932 to be replaced by Burton's shop.

Manchester Road, c. 1912. The buildings on the right were the Old Red Lion, Duckworth's tobacconists, Eastwood offices and Holdsworth's butchers with Walter Senior's barbers pole on the corner of Red Lion Street. On the left was the Bull Hotel. The shops on St James's Street were Addison's wine merchants, Dunkerley's boots and shoes and Allen and Hollely's drapers.

Joseph Harrison's cloggers, Sandygate, 1930s. Joseph was one of many cloggers who had their own business working in small shops. Cloggers made and repaired clogs, shaping the wooden soles and heels with long knives and cutting and stitching the leather uppers. Irons were fixed to the sole and heel, 'he would put Colne irons onto the collier's clogs and local irons onto the weaver's. The ones on the dole got by with car tyres cut to shape'.

Bell's, Manchester Road, c. 1890. The business was started in around 1848 by Sarah Bell and her brother. The shop was on the corner of Grimshaw Street until it relocated to numbers twenty-eight and thirty next door, the original site being occupied by a bank. In 1896 the shop was advertised as a draper, silk mercer, hatter, hosier, glover, furrier, milliner and dressmaker.

John Taylor's wines and spirits, *c.* 1909. John had moved to this site in around 1860 and was shortly to move again to another shop in Church Street. John started trading as a grocer in the 1840s and soon was supplied with wines and spirits from a firm in Liverpool. By 1865 John was sending a wine list to customers: 'I issue this little work – not as a contribution to your waste paper casket, but for serving you with some information upon a question which has of late occupied the brains of scientific men, "what shall we drink without injuring our health".' A lifelong friendship was formed with John Allen & Co. of Liverpool. John probably contributed the window display of an oxen pulling a cart of casks. The display dates from the 1870s and is in Towneley Hall's collection.

Four

Housing

Rose Cottage, Todmorden Road. In the 1850s, the cottage had a relatively large garden and summer house. Robert Simpson and his wife moved to the cottage in around 1892 where they celebrated their silver wedding anniversary. The Simpsons lived there until around 1920, when a previous occupant returned.

Gawthorpe Hall, *c*. 1890. The hall was built in the early 1600s and was the home of the Shuttleworth family. They were one of the major landowners in the area and in 1850 the hall was altered for Sir James Kay-Shuttleworth by architect Sir Charles Barry. The tower was raised, the interior restored and a formal garden laid. Sir James's granddaughter, the Hon. Rachel Kay-Shuttleworth (many knew her as 'Miss Rachel') lived at the hall most of her life. She was both a teacher and collector of embroidery and her collection at Gawthorpe is nationally known.

Ormerod House, c. 1920. The house was occupied by John Hargreaves until his death in 1834 and then by Revd William Thursby and successive generations. The Thursbys contributed to parkland, gardens, housing, a convalescent home, and church extensions as well as improving conditions for coal miners they employed. The house was demolished in 1947 following subsidence.

Ormerod House. The interior was a mixture of antique and modern furniture. The chair on the left of the fireplace dates from 1689 and was possibly made locally. Above the fireplace are portraits of Eleanor Mary, daughter of Colonel John Hargreaves (centre, of Hargreaves Collieries) and wife of Revd William Thursby (right). A copy of Thursby's portrait is in St John's Church, Worsthorne.

Royle Hall. Much of the hall was built by Nicholas Townley, of another branch of the Towneley family. The male line died out and Anne married into the Parker family to become Townley Parker. The Hall remained empty after the death of Canon Arthur Townley Parker in 1902 and may have been partly demolished in 1915. A local solicitor lived there as a tenant until 1929. The last of the ruins were bulldozed into the cellars shortly after the Second World War.

Oakbank, Todmorden Road, c. 1880. Built in around 1850, occupants included James and William Thompson who bequeathed and gave money for building Thompson Park and the William Thompson Recreation Centre. Large houses were built in the Todmorden Road and Brooklands area, along with those on Colne, Manchester and Padiham Roads.

Extwistle Hall, Briercliffe. Extwistle was the home of the Parker family, landowners in Briercliffe. It was one of a number of larger houses built for the local gentry and, with the attached cottages, formed one of the small settlements in Briercliffe. The Parkers moved away from the area in the early eighteenth century and the hall was leased to various tenants. The hall was damaged in 1862 and partly rebuilt. The building remained empty for a number of years and, although sold in 1987, it currently remains empty.

Barcroft Hall. The hall was lived in by the Barcroft family who built the house in the late sixteenth and early seventeenth century. Legend says there was a curse on the family and the male line would die out, which in fact it did in 1668. From 1696 the hall was tenanted. It remained in a semi-rural setting and as late as 1873, it was described as being in a 'beautiful landscape'. Barcroft was once owned by the Towneleys and Lady O'Hagan considered moving there after Towneley Hall was sold to Burnley Corporation.

Whittlefield House. Probably the most famous resident was George Slater, the mill owner, who built Clock Tower mill and Slater Terrace on Sandygate. Whittlefield was lived in by the Slater family until the 1920s. In around 1961, the property was purchased by Ernie Hall, who opened the Whittlefield House Club in 1964. The club became known as the 'Ponder' or 'Ponderosa'. The house was demolished in around 1976.

Treacle Row, *c.* 1890. The cottages were originally known as Further Row but were given the name Treacle after some cottages already with this name were demolished further down Coal Clough Lane. St Matthew's church was destroyed by fire on Christmas Day, 1927, 'we left the Christmas party to go and watch. The street were covered with snow and the flames lit up the stained glass windows'.

Colne Road. No date is recorded for this photograph but there are various methods the local historian can use to date a photograph. There is housing on both sides of the road, a chapel is on the right and a chapel-like structure on the left behind the cart. An adjoining street with a letter box is on the left and electric trams are in use. A visit to the street today shows that many of these buildings remain. Housing on the right is called Knightsbridge with a date stone of 1890 and the initials 'J.R.' The chapel-like building on the same side of the road has been demolished. The chapel on the left has the faint words Ebenezer Schools under the clock face. The large house at the road junction (Elm Street) is called Elm House (formerly Bankfield Villas) and the letter box has been replaced by a more modern one. Building plans date Ebenezer Schools as 1871, Bankfield Villas as 1878, and Knightsbridge as 1888-1890, laid out by John Rawlinson (J.R.). Trade directories show John lived in the block and cotton manufacturers lived in Bankfield Villas. Maps indicate the letter box was *in situ* between 1893 and 1912. Newspaper articles show electric trams were operating by 1902. Therefore, the photograph dates from between 1902 and 1912. Fashion can be used to date the photograph further. People on the right are wearing older fashions than those on the left. So using various sources and studying the image we can date the photograph to around 1905.

Cannon Street, Wapping, looking to the Market Hall, *c.* 1890. Wapping was the area bounded by Bridge Street, St James's Street, Hall Street and the River Brun. The building on the right was once a private house which was later converted to the 'Black Dog' inn. The area was prone to flooding, as shown by the two floodlines below the gas lamp.

Cannon Street, Wapping, looking towards Hall Street, *c.* 1895. The area was fashionable at one time but Wapping became one of the worst slum areas in the town. A ballad of 1850 described the area as:
'*The refuge of the desolate
The strong hold of the bad
And home of many great events
The child without a dad'*.

Malt Kiln Street, Hill Top. The housing at Hill Top, off Church Street, was one of the areas which was considered to 'require supervision' in 1919. Dr Thomas Holt reported that there were 'narrow and irregular streets and courts, badly lighted rooms and indifferent sanitary arrangements'. Malt Kiln Street was demolished in 1933, to be replaced with Council houses at Bleak House and Casterton.

Church Street, early 1900s. Jack Holt owned the cottage as well as 'a knacker yard and he sold horse meat from the front door. I often went round for horse meat "for the cat". I never remember us having a cat'. The property was demolished in 1938. The date stone is in Towneley Hall's collection.

Trafalgar Street from the junction of Whittaker Street, *c.* 1915. William Greenwood's newsagent, owned by 'Blind William', was one of a number of shops on Trafalgar Street including butchers, a tripe shop, confectioners and grocers. Many had living quarters above the street. Terraced housing occupied the streets such as Albion Street, Derby Street, Sandygate which ran uphill to the left.

Trafalgar Street from the junction with Sandygate. Although houses were on the street, the straightness and length made it seem that Trafalgar had 'cotton mills from one end to the other. The cotton workers used to take sandwiches for breakfast and dinner. We used to stand at the mill gates asking them if they had any bread left. Sometimes we would get some with meat or boiled ham'.

Healey Wood, early 1900s. Housing was built close to the workplace. A large number of mill workers and colliers lived in Healey Wood. Terraced housing here was an improvement compared with older housing in the town. The housing was built on a slope to help drainage, although sanitation remained basic and few houses had gardens.

Oxford Road, 1880s. The canal was a barrier to expansion. As a result, the area around Oxford Road and in Burnley Wood only developed in the second half of the nineteenth century. As in many other areas, such as Whittlefield and Stoneyholme, a separate community was created within the town. There were factories, shops, pubs, churches, chapels, 'chippies' and a nearby cinema. Many people had no reason to travel to the town centre, except on a special occasion.

Council housing, c. 1937. The first council houses were built on Towneley smallholdings in around 1909. During the 1920s and 1930s there was a massive increase in building when Rosehill, Stoops, Casterton and Bleak House estates were built. For many 'it was like reaching the promised land. The house was bitterly cold and the toilet was outside but there was a garden. A disused pit was just behind our house. What a playground'.

Towneley Park and Brunshaw, early 1900s. The hill on the right was laid out as the Brunshaw estate. Previously the land was used for poultry-keeping. The first poultry show was held in 1858 and the Utility Poultry Movement was founded in 1895. Poultry-keeping was especially popular with miners. The town was a poultry centre, especially between 1918 and 1939 when some men opened small poultry farms as an alternative to factory work.

Five

Work

Thomas Nutter's confectionery works, Bread Street. Founded in 1870, Thomas's speciality was 'lime fruits' although the firm made a range of sweets including 'malt and butter', 'tangerine oranges' and 'lemonade de luxe'. As with many other trades, the product was delivered using a horse and cart.

Clifton, Stoneyholme, Daneshouse, March 1935. This open area of land was built upon with housing and the motorway. Mills and factories followed the line of the Leeds-Liverpool canal (behind the gasworks) to the right, past the terraced housing and on to Bank Hall. Immediately to the left of the terraces was a ginny track (see p. 104) carrying coal from Clifton Colliery to the canal.

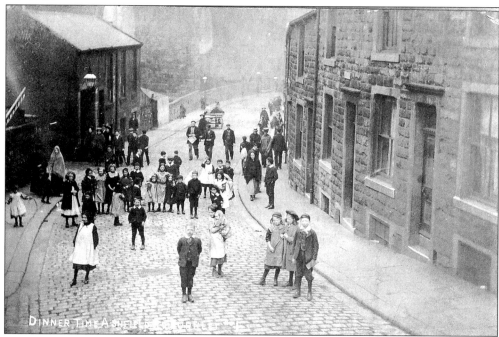

Dinner time, Ashfield Road, c. 1908. Many workers went home during their lunchtime break if their house was close enough. Clogs and shawls, worn by many in the photograph, were synonymous with the cotton industry. Until the 1920s older children worked 'half time', 'I started work in a mill when I was twelve years old. I used to work in the mornings one week, in the afternoons the next. I went to school for the rest of the time'.

Oxford Mill, Oxford Road, c. 1890. Cotton-spinning mills were usually multi-storey with large windows. In comparison, weaving sheds were single-storey with a north-light roof. Spinning mills suffered competition from larger mills in the 'spinning belt' of South Lancashire but many remained working into the 1900s.

Looming area, Elm Street Mill, 1920s. Weaving mills had a looming or drawing-in area where cotton was prepared before being taken into the weaving shed. The cotton warps were pulled through or drawn-in through the healds and reeds of a loom by a skilled man using simple tools.

Weaving shed, *c.* 1912. In the nineteenth century, cotton weaving surpassed spinning as the town's main industry. Weaving mills were built with preparation areas, warehousing and weaving sheds. The sheds were built as single-storey with north-light roofs and were designed to hold as many looms as possible. As a result, they appeared cramped with narrow alleys between looms and driving-belts. Unusually, this view was half of a stereoscopic photograph, giving a three-dimensional effect when seen through a special viewer.

Perseverance Mill, Padiham, *c.* 1909. A mill's interior was sometimes decorated with flags and banners to celebrate coronations, peacetime and weddings, as at Perseverance Mill shown here. Christmas was also a special time in some mills with 'rum and coffee, pies and a kissing rush. God help you if you were shy but how nice if someone you liked got in a free kiss'.

Weaving department, Technical School, c. 1895. The school was opened in Elizabeth Street in 1892, with accommodation for four hundred students; with joinery, plumbing and weaving classes it was felt the school would complement the art classes held in the Mechanics Institute. A new Technical Institute was opened in Ormerod Road in 1909.

Gertrude Steele and James Holmes, c. 1916. Gertrude was an art student at the Technical Institute in Ormerod Road. James taught for thirty years and retired as head of the weaving department in 1923. As well as being an authority on natural history, his books, including *Cotton Cloth Design* and *Manuscript Notes on Weaving*, were regarded as standard works. Between 1902 and 1912, his students won all but nine of the County Council scholarships to the Manchester School of Technology.

Barbara Melvin, cotton queen. Barbara worked at a mill in Padiham and was elected cotton queen in 1932. This was a competition introduced in the 1930s. Millworkers chose a queen from their town to represent them in a final at Blackpool, where a Lancashire queen was chosen. The queen's role was to raise the profile of the cotton industry, attempting to bring work back to Lancashire during a period of decline.

Platers and Stampers kitchenware factory, 1938. The town's rates were used to help pay for the building of the Colne Road factory, intended to try and offset the decline in the textile and related engineering industries. The name Prestige was acquired in the 1950s and it became synonymous with high quality kitchenware. Two of the most famous products were the 'Lancashire Peeler' and 'Miracle 885' can-opener. The 150 millionth 'Miracle' was presented to Burnley Council in 1990. The Prestige works closed in 1997.

Revd Thomas Williams at Butterworth & Dickinson's foundry, Liverpool Road, *c.* 1909. While curate at All Saints, Habergham, Thomas was involved with 'a social experiment' at the factory. He organized a lending library and a series of lectures during the lunch breaks. Men were encouraged to give some of the talks on subjects such as mutual improvement, first aid and objective thinking. Thomas was involved with other social concerns, particularly with the unemployed and in organizing trips and holidays.

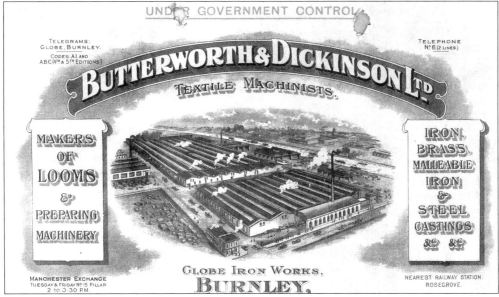

Letterhead, Butterworth & Dickinson's foundry, 1918. The textile industry was supported by engineering firms making preparation machinery and looms; among the largest in the town was Butterworth & Dickinson. The name was adopted in 1872 but they were also known as 'Butts and Dicks'. As well as allowing the 'social experiment' in the factory the firm also had football, cricket, swimming and cycling teams.

Waterside Mill, Rosegrove, November 1934. The former cotton mill was occupied by Burnley Components (Burco). The firm had made munitions during the First World War but moved to Waterside to increase production of their electric wash-boilers. A year later, the Corporation encouraged manufacturers to relocate and use empty mill property, through their 'Burnley Means Business' campaign.

Testing department, Waterside Mill, November 1934. By the 1930s, Burco supplied virtually all wash-boilers hired by local authorities in England and Wales. They also increased their share of the market in private properties, laundries, bakeries, dairies and soapworks. So much so, it was proclaimed: 'worldwide washday worries solved in Burnley'.

Laying the foundation stone, Hurstwood Reservoir, October 1911. Originally, Shorey Well by the River Brun was one of the main sources of drinking water. Increasing population led to a rise in demand and supplies were brought from reservoirs at Heckenhurst, Swinden and Cant Clough. A new site was chosen at Hurstwood in preference to Thursden and the reservoir was completed in 1923.

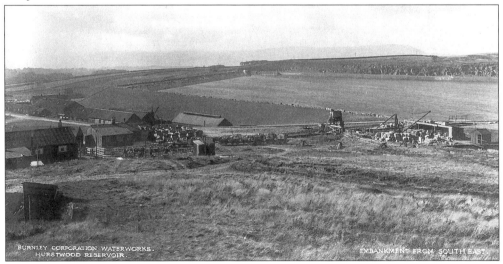

Constructing Hurstwood Reservoir. In 1911, over 300 people were working at Hurstwood, many of them living in small huts. Despite afforestation schemes on completion, the site was described in the 1940s as 'one of stark wilderness and utter loneliness. The scene might be pitched a thousand miles from a loom or shop'.

Bridge End Brewery, Westgate, c. 1880. The site dates from around 1720 but it was the Massey family who developed it into the town's largest brewery with pubs throughout East Lancashire. The firm introduced its owl trademark in 1937, claiming a drink of their beer was a 'wise choice'. The brewery was demolished in the 1970s.

Well Hall Brewery, Church Street. Operated by the Grimshaw family, the Well Hall or Keirby was the second largest in the town, brewing 'sparkling' ales. The maltings was on Church Street and the tower, built in around 1866, was a prominent feature. The brewery was taken over by Massey and eventually demolished in 1938.

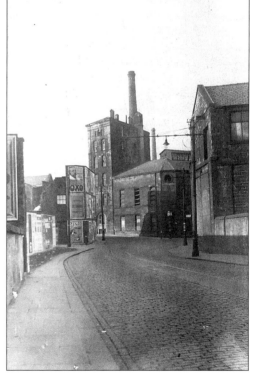

Police Force, 1893. The Borough force was established in 1887 with a total of sixty-seven men serving under Joseph Harrop, the first Chief Constable. Their early work was in dealing with theft and drunkenness, with some patrols in areas such as Wapping conducted in pairs for safety. From 1888-1955 the police station was in the Town Hall, where a number of cells remain in the basement.

The new police station, c. 1953. As early as 1909, a report criticised the facilities the police had available. A new police station and magistrates court was opened in September 1955. This replaced the station at the Town Hall where it 'was grim and unsatisfactory with inadequate space for interviews, and records could not be kept conveniently'.

Fire Brigade, Manchester Road. Until 1891, the brigade was run by volunteers under the command of Christopher Slater (on the right behind the front row). Most members lived near the new fire station which had been built in Manchester Road in 1881. Two steam-operated engines bought in the 1880s were named after the Rivers Calder and Brun; the *Brun* is probably pictured here. In 1891, the police took over the operation of the brigade.

Lodge Mill fire, October 1905. The mill was built for cotton-spinning on the banks of the Leeds-Liverpool canal at Reedley. Many mills burnt down. Despite having a sprinkler system in the mill and being close to the canal for water pumps, the combination of cotton, oil, grease and wooden floors meant that 'the fire king could reign... he had reduced the mill to a gigantic heap of smouldering wood, red hot stones and wrecked machinery'.

Boiler explosion, March 1892. The boiler exploded from a soapworks in Canal Street, flew across the river and landed in a bedroom at the Cross Keys Inn. A report suggested that a poorly-trained young boy had been left in charge of the boiler and the explosion was the result.

Towneley Colliery. The first sod was cut in 1869 by Alice Mary Towneley (Lady O'Hagan). The colliery was run by Brooks & Pickup, who also owned the adjacent fireclay works. As well as manufacturing water filters the firm also made bricks, pipes and sanitary ware, in competition with the more successful James Duckett.

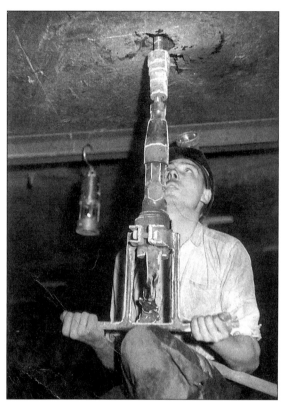

Jimmy Wormell, Reedley Colliery, 1950s. The colliery was sunk in 1879 and was the first in the area to have pit-head baths, paid for by the Thursby family. Reedley was used for testing new equipment such as roof bolts which Jimmy can be seen fixing in place here to support the roof.

Canal basin, Bank Hall Colliery. The colliery was opened in the 1860s and became the largest in the town. Bank Hall was famous for 'coal balls' or 'bobbers' (fossilized remains found when the coal was dug). Coal was transported by barge from the basin, by ginny track and a mineral railway which skirted Thompson Park on the way to the main railway line. Bank Hall closed in 1971 and the site was landscaped.

Sheepdog trial, Crow Wood Farm. Local trialling started at Worsthorne in 1902 and was resumed on land at Crow Wood Farm after the First World War. Organized by the Burnley Sheepdog Trials Society, profits went to the Victoria Hospital. The society was honoured in 1924 by having a cot named after it in the children's ward.

Holden, Briercliffe-with-Extwistle, c. 1890. Built as a farmhouse in the late sixteenth or early seventeenth century, it may have been occupied by a young member of the Parker family (see p. 55). In the 1840s the farmhouse was divided into three or four dwellings. The surrounding land was used for arable crops and pastoral farming. The farmhouse was the last in the district to have a cheese press *in situ*.

Edward Robinson, bellman c. 1872. Edward was appointed by the Towneley family in 1848 to ring a handbell and announce news, property sales and the names of lost children. He claimed to remember a time when one pig gave a week's supply of pork to all the butchers' shops and to know all the families in the town. His bell is in Towneley Hall's collection.

Work outing, c. 1922. The outing was a tradition enjoyed by many employees. Buses or charabancs were hired, as in the case of Ralph Mason's (tripeworks), to visit such places as Blackpool or Windermere. The expense was usually met by the employers. Outings were also arranged to celebrate special occasions such as a mill anniversary.

Six
Lowerhouse Printworks

Bleach house, Lowerhouse Printworks, 1883. The use of chlorine bleaches meant a change from open-air bleaches to works with internal bleaching-tanks. The works at Lowerhouse used cotton woven in the town ('Burnley Printers') from local firms including Haslam's, Tunstill's and J.D. & Bros (John Dugdale & Brothers, the earlier owners of the site).

A painting of Lowerhouse Printworks, *c.* 1830. The site was in almost continuous production from around 1795 until the 1960s. The factory was built for cotton-spinning by Peel, Yates & Co. and then taken over by the Dugdales, in around 1813, who introduced calico-printing soon after. The Dugdale family also built a new cotton mill to the east and were largely responsible for developing Lowerhouse as a mill village. New owners Alexander Drew & Sons ran the printworks from 1872 until the 1960s. Looking from Schole Bank, this is the earliest industrial view of Burnley. The original water-powered part of the works is behind the chimney on the left with early nineteenth-century spinning mills on the right. Housing at Long Row (Bear Street) is on the left with a large house in the centre at the bottom of the slope.

Daniel and Rhoda Drew in the garden at the printworks, 1883. The Drew family business was established by Alexander at Dalmanoch Printworks, Alexandria, near Glasgow. Alexander's sons, Daniel, Thomas and Alexander, ran the factory in Lowerhouse. Daniel was responsible for production and his brothers for the commercial side, with offices in Glasgow and Manchester.

The bellhouse and footpath entrance, 1882. Although there was a clock on site, this was removed when extensions were made in the 1880s. The bell was still used to 'keep time' in the early 1900s. Many of the workers lived nearby but some, especially skilled ones such as engravers and pentagraphers, had been recruited from other factories at Accrington. A gatehouse was built in 1880 and any employees who were late had their names entered into a book kept in the gatehouse.

The top of the brick foundation for the new chimney, 15 April 1885. Steam power had been introduced in the early nineteenth century when two beam engines were installed, one made by Ingham of Burnley. On the west of the site, the old square chimney was replaced by this circular one in 1885. At the same time new boilers were bought and a boiler house extended.

The new chimney, May 1885. The firm was always trying to make improvements and the new chimney was one of them. By 1888, many of the old dilapidated buildings had been restored and modern machinery had been introduced. Electric light in the old mill was introduced in the late nineteenth century and full electric drive in 1927. Silk screen-printing was developed in the 1950s.

The new chimney, June 1885. Business had been difficult in the first few years of the Drew's occupation in 1872 and Daniel was advised by his father that 'our production is much too small and should be double. I wish all your machinery and apparatus or whatever stands in the way of quantity put right'. Production increased from 1876-1889 and ten new trademarks were registered between 1885 and 1889.

The finished chimney. The 1880s saw the start of a period of great prosperity for the firm. Daniel visited European printworks on three separate trips in the 1880s and close relations were formed with Schlieper & Baum of Elberfeld, Germany. Visits were continued by his son John who was encouraged by Daniel to learn as much as possible: 'there is a style we have never done here, called manganese bronze, Schliepers used to do a lot of it. I would like you to become acquainted with it'.

A printing machine, 1880s. Originally, printing had been done by hand using blocks but machines meant quicker printing. A new printing shed was built in 1876. Engraving the patterned rollers and colour mixing was carried out in a separate part of the factory. The Drews also tried to improve dyeing and printing methods but were unsuccessful at this time.

A shipper's ticket. Cloth was exported worldwide with markets in Africa, India, the Far East and South America. Finished goods were packed with labels, some of which had the Drews' own trademark. Others had merchants' marks. The design sometimes contained a cultural reference to the country of destination. This refers to a Chinese story about finding horseshoe-shaped treasure.

The printworks, 1888. Daniel lived with his wife and family in the house, located in the middle of the works. The house had been extended in 1886 and included large gardens and a tennis court (near the gasholder); it remained in a semi-rural setting with a farm on the left. Open land was nearby, with footpaths at Jacky Wood, Knotts and Molly Wood.

Haytime, Jacky Wood, 1912. Behind the cart is the printworks and in the distance Dugdale's Lowerhouse mill. Daniel is on the left having just finished photographing his family in the hay field; helping to gather in the crop was often an annual family activity.

Lowerhouse Lodge, 1901. Water from several lodges was used in large amounts in the printworks for the various processes. The last and largest lodge to be built was the 'top' lodge in 1878. Daniel noted that 'the new reservoir began to fill from a heavy thunder shower on Saturday 18 May 1878. Water came over on Sunday at 5.30p.m.' The top lodge was also used by Burnley swimming club for practice races, skating, for weekend picnics and by workers who had a swim during their lunch break. The Drews were keen sailors and yachtsmen. The young boy sailing the boat is probably John, one of Daniel's sons; the boat may have been made by Daniel. John became a director of the company but a second son, Alan, was killed in action on the Western Front in 1915.

Seven

War

A fundraising indicator, Church Street, 1941. Painted by Alf Smith of Coal Clough, this recorded the town's efforts for a fundraising week. Towns were involved in many campaigns during the Second World War, such as 'Salvage', 'Dig for Victory', 'Warship Week', 'Spitfire Week' and 'Salute the Soldier'.

General Sir James Yorke Scarlett, *c.* 1869. James (second from the right) was an unlikely hero of the Crimea War. He successfully led the charge of the Heavy Brigade against a superior Russian cavalry force in October, 1854. He lived at Bank Hall with his wife Charlotte. Although unsuccessful as the Conservative parliamentary candidate in the town's first election in 1868, he was well respected in Burnley. When he died in 1871, the funeral route to Holme was lined with thousands of mourners.

The town cannons, Colne Road. They were given to the town in 1867. Some children used this area to play, 'we used to go down to a form in front of the cannons with pins which we crossed and made into shapes. We placed them on tram lines. The trams ran over them and they came out flat'. The cannons were removed for wartime scrap in 1941.

Cottage homes, Salus Street. These were opened by Princess Louise in 1905. They were built on land given by public benefactor Sir John O.S. Thursby in memory of the men of the East Lancashire Regiment who lost their lives in the Boer War (1899-1902). They were part of a national scheme to provide rent-free regimental homes for disabled soldiers. One was designed for a married couple with a small family, the other for four men.

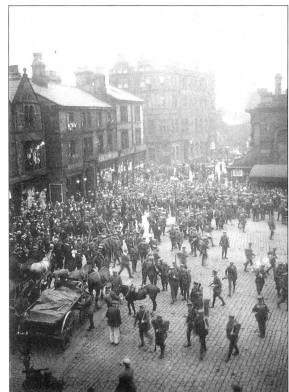

Howe Street (Market Place), August 1915. This was almost certainly a visit of the 'Accrington Pals' battalion of the East Lancashire Regiment, on a recruitment march before going to Ripon camp. Recruited from towns including Burnley, the battalion fostered a sense of comradeship and loyalty as men joined from the same street, factory or club.

Henry (Harry) Riley, *c.* 1916. Henry was the leader of Burnley Lads' Club which was established as a recreational and educational club for working-class boys. Over seventy members immediately followed Henry, when he joined the army, into the Burnley Company of the 'Accrington Pals'. He led two platoons in the Somme attack (1 July 1916) and was killed. He has no known grave but his name is recorded on the Thiepval Memorial. As a memorial to Henry, the town raised £3,000 by public subscription to pay off the Lads' Club's debt.

Robert Layfield. Robert rejoined the army when war was declared in 1914. He was killed in action serving in the Scottish Rifles at Loos in September 1915. Robert was a former member of the Lads' Club and, along with his brother Harold, is one of the 123 members recorded on the Lads' Club memorial. Their motto was 'Dare all but Dishonour'.

A flower bed, Queens Park, October 1915. This was designed by the head gardener James Bailey who had also been responsible for laying out Ightenhill Park. His design was the badge and motto of the East Lancashire Regiment (ELR). Many of the local men joined the ELR. Two other flower beds in the park were planted in the design of the Army Service Corps and the Royal Army Medical Corps.

Jennie Jackson ('Young Kitchener'), St James's Street, c. 1915. Jennie's motto was 'Tommy Atkins first, pleasure afterwards' and she was very successful at raising money for the war effort. Her greatest achievement was the purchase of a motor ambulance. Other children who raised money included Amy Foster ('Hieland Lassie'), and Edgar and Annie Wharf who sold golliwogs for a newspaper fund.

Bank Hall Hospital, c. 1914. Bank Hall was one of three military hospitals used in the town during the First World War. Matron Clara Frost (front row, centre) supervised the care of the sick and wounded, for which she was awarded the Royal Red Cross. In 1920, Bank Hall became a maternity hospital with accommodation for eight beds, 'with swinging cots at the foot for the accommodation of his majesty, the baby'.

Huntroyde Hospital. A second military hospital was at Huntroyde. Part of the home was used between 1914 and 1917, due to the generosity of the Starkie family. Soldiers were treated by a doctor from Padiham and resident nursing staff. Although at Huntroyde a short time, many seemed to enjoy their stay. One soldier wrote: 'Eh Jimmy! look at stuff. The remark most often on our lips owing to the remarkable quality of the large stock of the above article sometimes called fluff (young women) available in the Padiham district'.

Unveiling Hapton War Memorial, February 1921. Memorials erected after the First World War varied in their style, construction and location. Hapton's was built by public subscription next to the school on Manchester Road. Included on the memorial is William Stephenson, one of thirty-nine local men in the Royal Army Medical Corps who were lost at sea when the *Royal Edward* sank in August 1915.

Home Guard, *c.* 1943. The Home Guard was originally called the Local Defence Volunteers. They were volunteers who would become part of the armed forces in the event of invasion. Exercises were held, as in 1941 when Nelson 'attacked' Burnley. One attacker 'entered a house at the moment a domestic row was at its height. The presence of an armed soldier did nothing to modify the fury of the battling wife who hurled a slab of margarine at her husband's head'.

Towneley Hall, sandbagged c. 1943. During the early years of the Second World War, the great fear was air and gas attack and precautions were taken against both. These included establishing a network of firewatchers, ARP posts and exercises to simulate aerial attacks. Captured German maps show the main targets were the railway sidings at Rosegrove and industrial sites along the canal. Only one bomb was dropped in central Burnley, in Thompson Park.

Freedom of the Borough, East Lancashire Regiment, June 1953. Over 1,000 men marched with 'colours flying, drums beating, bands playing and bayonets fixed', the traditional privileges of Freedomship. The event coincided with celebrations for the Coronation and for the ninth anniversary of D-Day. The Regiment amalgamated with the South Lancashire to form the Lancashire Regiment in 1958.

Eight

Transport

Towneley Station, *c.* 1890. This engine was built in 1883 and was regularly used on the Todmorden line (opened in 1849) serving the small urban communities. The station suffered increased competition from buses and finally closed in 1953 when only a few passengers regularly used the train service.

Jim Redford (left) was a familiar sight driving the steam engine *Mazzeppa* on the railway to Todmorden. He lived near the railway and was worthy of a tribute in Henry Nutter's *Local Rhymes*:
'I've not the slightest dread indeed,
With thee I've nought to fear
The welcome to thy puffing steed,
Old Jim the engineer'.

Railway viaduct, Caldervale, July 1908. Large cracks and damage to the viaduct were the result when part of Greenhalgh's dyeworks fell into the river. An eyewitness said, 'I saw the building suddenly fall. It almost made my heart jump into my clogs did the sight'. Trains could not cross the viaduct and disruption was caused to the timetable during the local holiday.

Rosegrove Station, *c.* 1888. The original station, built in 1848 on the East Lancashire Railway, was unusual for having the main buildings on the down line. The station was close to the junctions for Padiham, Colne and Todmorden and was redeveloped in the late 1890s. An extensive network of sidings was added, the station buildings moved and rebuilt, and a motive power depot erected to house steam locomotives. In 1968, Rosegrove was one of the last sheds in Britain to operate steam locomotives.

Holme Station. The railway to Todmorden had steep gradients leading to the summit at Copy Pit. Drivers of heavy coal-trains had to be very skilful taking trains to and from Todmorden. Holme station was unusual because there were no goods facilities. Passengers were carried to the village and trippers to Thieveley Pike. The station closed in July 1930 because of competition from road traffic.

Holme Station After The Smash. 27.9.07. No 1.

The Smash at Holme Station, September 1907. This accident was the result of waggons becoming uncoupled, running down the gradient and crashing into the rear of the train at Holme. The train was carrying onions, coke and iron and thousands of onions were strewn over the area. William Pym, deputy stationmaster at Holme, was killed as a result of the collision.

Bridge Street, 1955. Manchester Road (opposite Bridge Street) was known as 'death hill' because of the frequency of runaways. This lorry, loaded with timber, had brake failure and it crashed into Waller & Richardson's shop on Bridge Street. The assistant noticed 'a mass of wood coming across the road. There was a crash like an earthquake and the whole building trembled. We all had lucky escapes'.

Deerplay toll bar, Cliviger. Four turnpike roads were built in Cliviger, replacing many of the ancient highways which crossed the area. Deerplay toll bar (used for payment between sections) was at the junction of the road to Waterfoot, on the 1817 Burnley-Rochdale turnpike. The toll bar was later used as a sweetshop when this area became a popular picnic site.

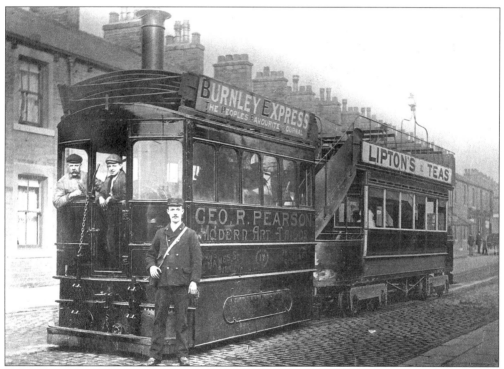

Steam tram, *c.* 1899. The steam tram network run by the Burnley and District Tramways was opened in 1881. It was the second to operate in Britain. The locomotive No. 12 and tramcar No. 14 were built at Loughborough in 1897. The journey times between Nelson and Burnley and Padiham and Burnley were both thirty minutes, but the gradients *en route* meant the top deck remained uncovered to reduce weight. The last steam tram ran in 1901.

Padiham bridge, 1905. The Corporation electric tram service to Padiham started in January 1902. The old bridge over the River Calder was rebuilt and widened. Car No. 21 was built in 1902 to carry seventy seated passengers.

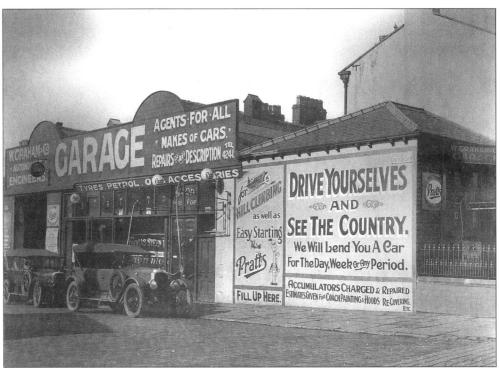

Simpson's garage, Parker Street. In 1882, the site was a harness room and coach house but was developed as a garage in the 1920s by Graham and Simpson to cater for an increasing number of cars in the early 1900s. Cars had the Burnley registration 'CW'. Occasionally, some were registered by owners with the same initials who lived outside Burnley such as Charles Webb from Stourbridge and Charles Wade from Cornwall.

Leeds-Liverpool Canal, from Knotts, looking towards Gannow, 1902. The Burnley section was built between 1796 and 1801. Factories were built along the banks to use water for their boilers as well as for transport. Goods carried included cotton, coal, flour and sugar. Despite competition from the railway, the canal could compete, since commercial traffic only ceased in 1963.

The culvert, 1885. The original bridge to carry the Leeds-Liverpool Canal over Eastgate (Yorkshire Street) was built in 1796. In 1896 and 1897 two 'gimlet holes' were bored either side of the central arch for pedestrians. In 1904, the tramway to Towneley was added and in 1926 a new culvert opened to widen the road.

The culvert, looking northwards, c. 1897. Repairs to the canal were needed after the addition of the two gimlet holes in Yorkshire Street. The culvert was halfway along the 'straight mile', the local description of the canal between Finsley Gate and Ormerod Road. This was one of the industrialized parts of the canal with a coal staithe (behind the barge), lime kilns, ropeworks and cotton mills along the banks. Rishton Mill, used for cotton-spinning, is on the left. Originally a sawmill of the 1840s, extensions were added such as the warehouse (in front of the chimney) in the 1860s and a tower for the sprinkler system in around 1890. The photographer of this view took a picture looking to Finsley Gate at the same time. The policeman on the left was obviously keen to be photographed as he appears in both views!

Finsley Gate bridge. The area near the canal, at this point, was commonly called 'Turnbridge' because of the nature of the bridge itself. The bridge was also known as 'Doctor's Bridge' after Dr Henry Parkinson who lived at Hollingreave House. The maintenance yard behind was one of several on the Leeds-Liverpool Canal. The ginny from Towneley Colliery (see p. 104) ended at a staithe to the right of the buildings.

Finsley Gate bridge. This temporary wooden bridge allowed access to Burnley Wood while a new permanent bridge was built and opened in 1885. The old bridge was removed because it was considered a danger and was insufficient to meet the needs of increased traffic to and from Burnley Wood.

'Marble Arch', Healey Wood, c. 1902. This name was used sarcastically to describe the path linking Springfield Road and Marlborough Street. The arch was removed in 1903 to improve communications between Healey Wood and Burnley Wood. The colliery tramway (or ginny) on top was one of several in the town. The ginny was used to transport coal in small trucks. This one ran from Towneley Colliery to the canal at Finsley Gate. When the arch was demolished the ginny was taken underground into a tunnel.

Nine

Playtime

Clarion cycling club, Crown Point, 1945. On a bitterly cold Good Friday, members were *en route* to a Clarion clubhouse in Wilmslow, Cheshire. Clarion cycling clubs were first established in 1894. The name was taken from the socialist newspaper and the club emphasized fellowship, outdoor pursuits and socialism. Shown in the photograph are, from left to right: Alice Pickup, Elsie ?, Ivy Ratcliffe, Betty Law, -?-. All were members of Burnley Clarion, which by 1945, was more a social than a political organization.

Clarion cycling club at Towneley Hall, 1912. The club had both male and female members, recognizing each other by a common call: 'next time you hear a comrade call "boots" don't look at him as though he was calling you something unpleasant, answer "spurs" and stop if you have time'. This photograph was used in a club calendar of cycle trips for 1914; destinations included Thorneyholme (with a sing-song), Twiston, Malham, as well as holiday runs. On Wednesday evenings there were 'propaganda' trips to spread the socialist message to local areas such as Hapton, Higham, Holme and Worsthorne.

Victoria cycling club, 1889. By the late 1880s, cycling was safer, easier and cheaper. Clubs such as the Victoria offered members the chance to buy bicycles by weekly subscription. The club was awarded various cups, including one for the largest number of cyclists attending a rally between 1888 and 1890.

William Salmon, trick cyclist from Rosegrove. William appeared in fêtes and music halls throughout Britain where his most famous tricks were on a single wheel. His last performance was in 1919 when he rode a wheel from Bank Hall to the town centre to celebrate the opening of the maternity hospital. He was also a recognized cyclist and his 'ordinary' bicycle (wrongly called a penny-farthing) is in Towneley Hall's collection.

Winners of the Lancashire Football Cup, 1890. The Burnley team which led the 'rout of the English cup holders' was, from left to right, back row: W. McFetridge, W.H. Bury, J. Kearsley (umpire), D. Spiers, E.T. White (secretary). Middle row: R. Haresnape, A. McLardie, A. Lang (captain), C. Lambie, A. Stewart, J. Hill. Front row: A. Kay, J. Keenan. The team beat Blackburn 2-0 with Stewart reputedly scoring both goals. The game was played at Accrington where 15,000 spectators watched Burnley's first appearance in any cup final. All 'except in Blackburn perhaps admitted that the best team won'. A band welcomed the team home with 'See the Conquering Hero Comes' and a reception was held at the Bull Hotel.

The FA Cup-winning team, April 1914. Burnley played Liverpool in the final at Crystal Palace with the only goal scored by Bert Freeman. He 'darted in like a flash of lightning and taking the ball before it touched the ground hooked it with his instep into the left hand corner of the net'. The train carrying the team home from Manchester had a specially decorated engine. Crowds cheered along the route. At stations including Blackburn, there 'were demonstrations of delight. Boyle and the Cup were in great request'. The team was met by huge crowds in the streets and the workers from at least one mill went on strike so as they could see the triumphant return.

Return of the FA Cup team, 1962. Burnley lost 3-1 to Tottingham in the final, with the Burnley goal scored by Jimmy Robson. The team was Blacklaw, Angus, Elder, Adamson, Cummings, Miller, Connelly, McIlroy, Pointer, Robson and Harris. A tour of the town followed their return, with one spectator dressed in wetsuit and goggles in the pouring rain.

Burnley cricket club. The first cricket match was played in 1828 at Bull Meadow (Hargreaves Street). Known originally as the Trafalgar Club, the team played at various venues until 1847, when a permanent site was found at Turf Moor. The old pavilion was extended in 1953 and replaced in 1968.

Burnley cricket club, 1908. The team won the Lancashire League in three successive seasons during the years 1906-1908. The players were, from left to right, back row: Dawson, Cudworth, Whittaker, Shackleton, Johnson, Bracewell. Front row: Cook (professional), Aspinall, Bell (captain), Crossley, Smith. The club's flag 'BCC' reputedly reflected the backbone of the team – Arthur Bell, Harry Cudworth and William Cook.

Thomas Roberts (and his wife), c. 1917. Along with 'Little Dick Boys of Trinity' (see p. 46), Thomas was one of the 'greats' of the cricket club in the 1870s. He was the best batsman and bowler of 1870 and the highest aggregate and average scorer for 1875. He was awarded a life membership in 1904.

Palace skating rink, Church Street. The Palace was opened in 1909, one of several rinks catering for the increased demand in roller skating. By 1927, it was both a dance hall and skating rink. It was the venue for the 'Whirlwinds', who were a troupe of roller skaters, the trainer put you in for a medal, if you passed you paid him. For your bronze medal you paid him ten bob, silver a pound, gold two pounds'.

Stepping stones, near Ightenhill. The stones across the River Calder became the cause of a legal dispute with the Starkie family, who eventually agreed to close the right of way only once a year. The area was popular for picnics and paddling, especially at weekends and Easter. They were replaced by a bridge, slightly upstream, in 1928. This in turn was replaced by a new bridge in 1980.

Springhill, *c.* 1889. The open spaces of Healey Heights were popular, being close to residential areas. Healey Heights was the town's 'first lung' or recreation area, especially popular with couples, 'we all went up Healey Heights, the local rendezvous and Annie showed us her bloomers. The outcome was I got a hell of a beating'.

The iron pipe at Heasandford. The pipe was a popular 'dare' for children to walk across. The walk along the banks of the River Brun through Heasandford was described in 1897 as 'the nicest walk about Burnley on account of the lovely scenery around. There are the green trees whose spreading branches invite the admiration of all who pass, there are the rocks standing high upon the banks and the grand old Brun rippling as though itself on pleasure bent'.

Lee Green reservoir, Roggerham. Roggerham was one of the smaller settlements in Briercliffe. The name is thought to derive from the personal name 'Roger'. The area was popular with walkers where 'nature has toned everything down - the houses, walls, fields, hills and moors look medieval and historic'. Behind is the Roggerham Gate Inn.

Tattersall Wilkinson. 'The Sage of Roggerham' was a noted antiquarian, historian, linguist and scientist. He was described as 'general instructor of all Mankind expounder of All arts and sciences both ancient and modern, purveyor of refreshments to the British public'.

114

The Literary and Philosophical Society, *c.* 1900. The group is shown here outside Scar House, Hill Top, their regular meeting place. The first attempt at forming the society was in 1861 but this had been unsuccessful. It was re-formed in 1893, and the group met at various places before settling on Scar House in 1894. A year later a lecture hall and exhibition room were established. The society was founded for the 'working man' (as opposed to the Literary and Scientific Society) and had both clerical and manual workers as members. Study collections included books, pamphlets, literature, history, science and natural history. The group also received sketches from Philip Gilbert Hamerton and Egyptian artefacts from Professor John Garstang of Liverpool.

Hurstwood village. The cottages are, from left to right: The Poplars, Brookside, Rose Cottage, Moorfell Farm. Although popular for a day trip, the village was a stop-off for some: 'the longest walk was Hardcastle Crags and back. Past Ormerod House to come out at Hurstwood village where you could get tea if you were better off. We always took our own bottles of water and food. Then onto Hardcastle Crags'.

Scout camp, July 1914. Five scout troops travelled by train to the Fylde coast for their annual camp. Four were at Ansdell and the YMCA troop at Bispham. The YMCA scouts earned various badges at camp for cooking and 'good turns', which included stopping a runaway horse. On their return, the scouts were put to war work, guarding telegraph wires.

Mechanics' Institute, Manchester Road. The 'Mechanics' was the town's social and cultural centre. It began in 1834 when a small club was formed by foundry workers. The club met in a cottage in the Meadows district. It was resolved that they should become an institute as soon as possible. A prospectus was issued in 1845 to erect a building for the 'instruction of the members in the principles of the useful and ornamental arts and in the various other branches of useful knowledge, together with their rational amusement and the cultivation of their tastes'. The foundation stone was laid by Charles Towneley in 1851. Designed by James Green, the Mechanics' was opened in 1855.

Statuary tableau, Mechanics' Institute, January 1907. Tableaux were a form of mime, creating pictures without movement, which were performed by students at the School of Art based at the Mechanics'. It was reported that 'there has never been a better set of tableaux. Japanese lanterns hung from the roof lit by electricity. Elsewhere prettily tinted hangings, floors covered with red baize, furniture prettily arranged'.

St Catherine's church choir, 1897. The church's foundation stone was laid in 1895. Originally, the name was to have been St Alban's but was changed in memory of Catherine Townley Parker, wife of the Rector of Burnley. The first incumbent was the Revd A.B. Edlestone from 1897-1918. The choir was one of a distinguished group of choral societies in the town.

Palace Theatre, St James's Street. The Palace was built in a matter of weeks in 1907 (faster it was said than a gentlemen's lavatory in Manchester Road). Originally owned by the MacNaughton Vaudeville Circuit, the Palace was both a theatre and cinema at various times until 1962. Then it became the Silver Dollar bingo hall. The building was demolished in 1973.

Grand Cinema, *c.* 1931. The Grand was built next to the Palace with a capacity of nearly 1,000 people. The first moving picture programme had been held at the Empire Theatre of Varieties in 1896 but it was the 'talkies' which boosted cinema audiences. The Grand closed in the 1950s; the last films were *Desert Legion* and *Above Us the Waves*.

Walking day, Fulledge chapel. Fulledge was opened for worship in 1861, with a Sunday school added two years later. In common with others, the chapel had a walking day 'with a band playing. We'd all have to be dressed in white. We used to parade through our local streets and then we'd go onto a field. Ladies would be busy putting cloths over trestles and boards. Buns came out – bun and coffee, it was lovely'.

Queen Victoria's Jubilee, 1887. The focus of celebrations was a procession by 7,000 schoolchildren from sixteen schools. In the morning they met in the Market Place and paraded along St James's Street, Westgate, Trafalgar Street and Manchester Road, returning to the Market Place. The children then dispersed. The afternoon was spent either having a 'bun and coffee' or playing games in fields.

Memorial Park, Padiham, May 1935. Selected children planted trees to celebrate King George V's Jubilee. Ten trees were planted including pyrus, malus, mountain ash, pink thorn and flowering cherries. Other events included children's sports at Worsthorne, a beacon on Crown Point, presentation to Wheatley Lane children of a Jubilee mug, and buns, coffee and sports at Briercliffe recreation ground. It seems that Nelson had no official celebrations for political reasons. Shown in the photograph are, from left to right: -?-, Annie Taylor, -?-, Ethel Hargreaves, Margaret Greenwood, Kenneth O'Hara, Fred Almond (tallest boy), Chatburn Duxbury, Amy Grimshaw (holding tree), Arthur Hitchon, Roy Packer (holding tree), Carol Roberts, Mary Phillipson, Jack Gee, Doreen Mouncy, Jack Heap, Irene Whittle, Freda Ashworth.

Site of Queens Park, *c.* 1891. Land was given to the Corporation by Sir John Hardy Thursby and the park was opened in July 1893. The original site 'presented few attractive features. It was a bare irregular slope with hardly a vestige of foliage'. The twenty-eight acres were planted with shrubs, laid out with walks and separate playgrounds for girls and boys. A colliery ginny track was hidden by planting schemes.

Scott Park, *c.* 1920. Alderman John Hargreaves Scott's will provided money for a public park which opened in August 1895. A memorial to John was unveiled in 1898 and a bust a year later. In 1901, children were heard arguing by an adult that 'Scott's likeness looked the other way. The other boys said it had never been turned round. The boy stuck to what he had said'. As an aside the adult commented 'perhaps his father is a Tory'.

The 'monkey rack', Scott Park, c. 1896. The park was laid out on part of the Hood House estate. Facilities only gradually developed with a bowling green in 1897, a children's playground in 1912 and a tennis court in 1925. The 'monkey rack' was a meeting place for courting couples.

Bank Hall estate. Looking towards St Peter's church, this was the site of the walks and Italian garden at Thompson Park. The land owned by the Thursby family stretched beyond Bank Hall and was used for various events before it was a park. The land was sold by the Thursbys to the Corporation for £3,000.

Building the boating lake, Thompson Park, 1920s. The park was built following the bequest of James Thompson who died in 1920. Fifty unemployed men were given over a year's employment when they laid out the park. It was opened in July 1930.

Boating lake, Thompson Park, 1930s. It was originally suggested the park should have an art gallery, museum, winter garden and aviary. When completed the park's special features were the Italian gardens, conservatory and lake. The boating lake was very popular. Over 4,000 people used the lake in three days in 1930. Park staff used megaphones to ask rowers to 'keep to the left' but there were many accidents.

Burnley Fair, July 1902. The fair dates from 1294 when a right to hold a market (or fair) was granted to landowner Henry de Lacy. The fair was commercial until the nineteenth century when amusements and entertainments began to appear. When the pleasure fair was held on the Cattle Market, Parker Lane in 1902, it was reported as 'the same old fair with pie stalls, photographic booths, hobby horses, merry go rounds with the organs attached emitting music of a character which can only be described as barbaric'. The fair was held in the holiday week when the factories closed. Virtually all shops were closed on the Tuesday and Wednesday, allowing even newsagents to go on the annual picnic.

Habergham Nuts, Isle of Man, *c.* 1908. The 'nuts' (young men) were a group on holiday at Cunningham's Camp. They would have chosen the name for their own tent, a custom at Cunningham's before the First World War. The camp catered for many male groups throughout the North of England and behind the tent was the dining room. The group was probably on holiday during Burnley Fair. Other people visited coastal resorts during local holidays such as Southport, 'they called the landlady Mrs Broadbent. My mother and dad used to go out every morning to buy whatever we were having for dinner or tea. We'd sit on the sands all morning, if you'd enough money you'd get an ice cream cornet'.

Carnival, September 1924. The carnival was organised by the Burnley branch of the Royal Ancient Order of Buffaloes to raise money for the Victoria Hospital and the Mayor's Fund for Children's Holiday Homes. The procession started at Ightenhill progressing through the town. Groups taking part included bands, Sunday schools, companies such as Redman's (grocers) and Nutter's (sweets) as well as individuals. Tacklers (loom mechanics) were typically self-mocking, 'they rested in peace suitably disposed over and around their machines. Their brains were in the dustbin marked full'.

Carnival boat, September 1932. The carnival on the Prairie fields was staged to raise money for the Victoria Hospital. The 'boat' was a decorated and illuminated tramcar from Queensgate Depot. Competitions were held and a street collection made, of which £3 was collected by Nelson Fire Brigade's dog. Tramcars and buses were often converted and decorated for events. Examples include a 'tank' used for fundraising in the First World War and an illuminated bus celebrating the Centenary of the Borough in 1961.

Yorkshire Street, 1890s. Important features of the town's history appear in this picture although it suffers from some deterioration through age. Most street scenes contain at least one chimney, reflecting the town's industrial growth. The tower is Rishton Mill. This spinning mill was served by two forms of transport, the canal and the horse. Two cloggers' shops, with their clog signs, are on either side of the street and two public houses are on the left. The people surprisingly seem unprepared for, and unaware of, the photographer.